Who Pooped
in the Park?

written by Gary D. Robson · illustrated by Elijah Brady Clark

FARCOUNTRY
PRESS

To my mother, who used to love taking me to
Rocky Mountain National Park. I miss you, Mom.

ISBN: 978-1-56037-320-9

© 2005 by Farcountry Press
Text © 2005 by Gary D. Robson

CIP data is on file at the Library of Congress.

Who Pooped in the Park? is a registered trademark of Farcountry Press.

For more information about our books, write Farcountry Press, P.O. Box 5630,
Helena, MT 59604; call (800) 821-3874; or visit www.farcountrypress.com.

Manufactured by:
Artron Art Co., LTD
No. 19 Shenyun Road
Nanshan District
Shenzhen, China 518053
in April 2021

Produced in the United States of America.

25 24 23 22 21   8 9 10 11 12

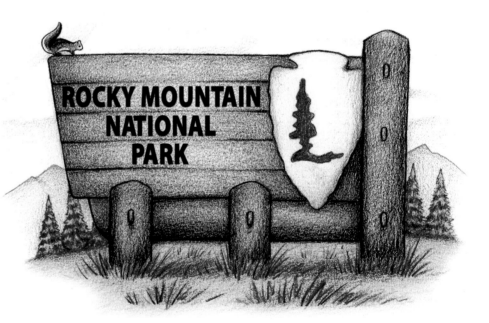

"Dad? I have to go to the bathroom." Michael squirmed in the back seat.

"We'll be at our campground in just half an hour," said Dad. "We're in Rocky Mountain National Park now."

3

"He's just nervous," said Michael's sister. "He thinks a bear's gonna eat him."
She growled at Michael and made her fingers look like claws.

"Stop it, Emily," said Mom. "Nobody is getting eaten by anything."

Michael was very excited about the trip, but Emily was right. He *was* nervous. He had just read a book about bears. He knew how big they could get, especially grizzly bears. And he was afraid that a hungry bear would eat just about anything—maybe even a boy.

"I *am* kind of scared of grizzly bears," admitted Michael.

"Don't worry," Dad told him. "There aren't any grizzlies in Colorado anymore. Just black bears. And we'll show you how to count a black bear's toes and never get close enough to be scared."

"Here's our campsite. Let's set up the tent. Then we can go for a walk and I'll show you what I mean," Dad said. Michael was awfully worried about bear toes, but tried not to show it.

"Let's hurry!" said Emily. "I want to see some animals!"

Once the tent was up, the whole family went for a hike. Emily started to complain before they even left the campground. "I haven't seen any animals yet. Maybe there aren't any here!"

"Sure there are," said Dad. "Let's see what we can learn about them from their *sign*."

"Sign?" said Michael. "You mean like sign at the zoo?"

"I'm talking about signs that the animal has been around. Look at the scat on that rock," said Dad.

"Scat?" asked Emily, looking a little less grumpy. "What's scat?"

"It's the word hikers and trackers use for animal poop," Dad replied.

"Another example of animal sign is tracks," said Mom.

"You mean footprints?" asked Michael. "Like these?"

"Very good," said Mom. "It looks like we've found signs of a marmot!"

The Straight Poop

Marmots live in high, rocky areas and often leave their scat on top of rocks.

"A *what?*" Michael wanted to know.

"A marmot," said Mom. "They're related to woodchucks. The ones you'll see around here are yellow-bellied marmots."

"See, Michael," said Dad. "We don't have to get up close to an animal to learn about it. Instead of a close encounter of the *scary* kind, we'll have a close encounter of the *poopy* kind."

Everybody laughed, and Mom made a gross-out face.

"Dad! Mom! Look over here! I found bunny scat!" yelled Michael. "It's just like what we have in Fluffy's cage."

"We came all the way to Rocky Mountain National Park for *that*?" grumbled Emily. "Michael's bunny makes plenty of poop at home."

The Straight Poop

This "bunny" is actually a snowshoe hare. It has wide feet to run on the snow, and its coat changes color with the seasons; snowshoe hares are white in the winter to blend with the snow.

14

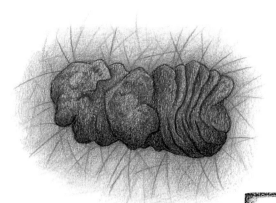

deer/elk scat: spring/summer

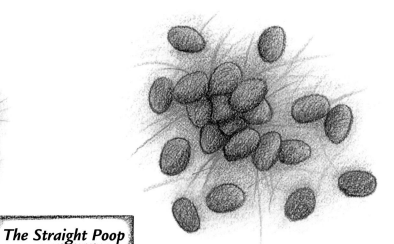

deer/elk scat: fall/winter

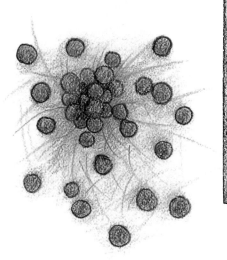

rabbit scat

jelly beans

The Straight Poop

Rabbits eat their own scat! They do this to get as much nutrition from their food as they can. The little balls you sometimes find are food that has been through twice.

"That's not from a rabbit," said Mom. "It's from a deer."

"Right! Bunny poop looks like little balls," added Dad. "Deer scat is shaped more like jelly beans."

"Are these deer tracks?" Michael asked.

"Yes!" said Mom. "See how they're split? They have hooves with two parts."

"What are these marks?" asked Emily. She was starting to get interested.

"Those are from its dew claws," said Mom. "They're little claws behind the hoof. Dew claws sometimes show in deer tracks in soft ground. Lots of other animals have dew claws, too, including cats and dogs."

dew claw

hoof

Female deer, elk, and moose don't grow antlers. Reindeer are the only members of the deer family in which both males and females have antlers.

"Oh, no!" said Michael. "Here's one of his antlers. Did a bear eat him?" Michael looked around nervously.

Dad bent down by the antler. "No, he's fine. Deer shed their antlers every winter and then grow a new, bigger set the next year. This antler is from a mule deer."

"But these tracks over here are bigger," said Mom, as she studied the ground. "They're from an elk, and it was in a hurry!"

Michael and Emily went over to look.

"How can you tell?" said Michael.

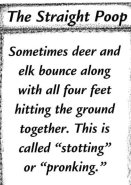

stotting
or
pronking

galloping   walking

"The hoofprints get very far apart here," Mom explained, "and the back prints are in front of the front prints."

"It was walking backwards?" said Emily.

"No, it was galloping. Something scared it, and it was moving fast."

"I know what scared it," Dad called.

The family hurried over to look.

"This is coyote scat," Dad said, "and there are coyote tracks all around here."

"They look like dog tracks," said Michael.

"That's because the coyote is a member of the dog family," explained Dad.

"There were a lot of coyotes around here," said Mom. "See how the adults left big tracks and the pups left smaller ones?"

"Their den is probably nearby. I'll bet they scared the elk away," Dad guessed.

"Did the coyotes get it?" Michael asked.

"I don't think so," said Mom. "Look!"

Far across the meadow, they saw a family of coyotes lying in the sun and watching a herd of elk.

As they walked along the trail into the woods,
Michael looked all over for tracks.

"Look, everyone! I found another coyote track."

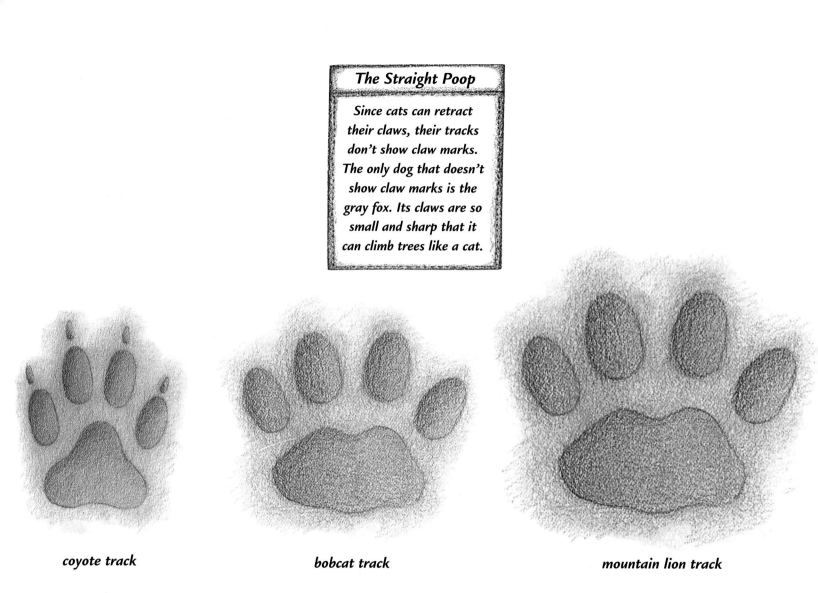

The Straight Poop

Since cats can retract their claws, their tracks don't show claw marks. The only dog that doesn't show claw marks is the gray fox. Its claws are so small and sharp that it can climb trees like a cat.

coyote track

bobcat track

mountain lion track

"That's not a coyote track," said Dad. "It doesn't show any claw marks, and the front of the big pad looks dented in."

"It's too big to be a bobcat track, so I'd say it's from a mountain lion," said Mom.

"Are they as big as panthers?" Michael asked, wide-eyed.

"Actually, that's another name for the same cat," Mom said with a smile. "Mountain lion, cougar, panther, painter, puma, and catamount are all names for the same animal!"

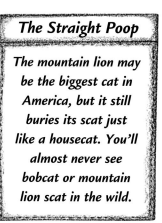

The Straight Poop

The mountain lion may be the biggest cat in America, but it still buries its scat just like a housecat. You'll almost never see bobcat or mountain lion scat in the wild.

mountain lion

bobcat

"Wow! There's a huge pile of scat right here in the middle of the trail," called Michael. "Is it from a mountain lion?"

"This scat couldn't have come from a meat eater like a mountain lion. It looks like it has grass and oats in it," said Dad.

The Straight Poop

Horses can walk while they poop, but they stop and stand still to pee.

"It's horse poop!" said Emily.

"Right," said Mom. "People ride horses up here. Let's see if we can find any tracks."

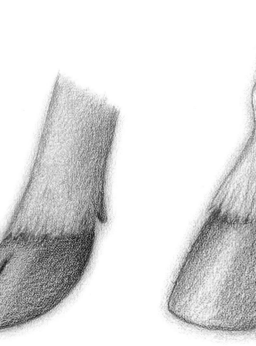

deer hoof

horse hoof

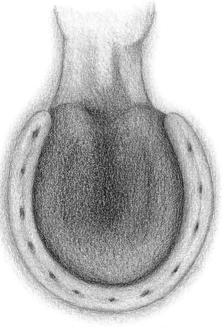

horse hoof with metal shoe

Michael found tracks, all right, but they didn't look like he expected.

"That's an awfully funny-shaped hoof," he said.

"Horses don't have split hooves like bison and deer," said Dad. "It's just one part."

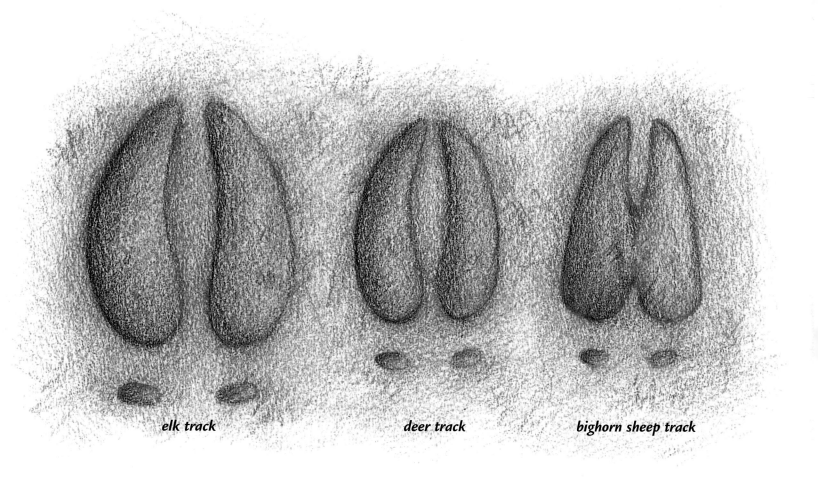

elk track *deer track* *bighorn sheep track*

"But these prints over here are split," said Emily.

"Yes," said Mom. "They're too small to be elk prints, and the sides are straight, not curved like elk and deer prints."

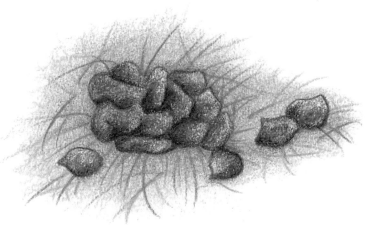

bighorn sheep scat

"Those are prints from a Rocky Mountain bighorn sheep," said Dad.

Michael and Emily looked around excitedly. Emily spotted them first. "There they are, up on the mountain!"

The Straight Poop

Bighorn sheep have hooves that grip rocks very well, making them excellent climbers.

"What are the white streaks on this tree?" asked Michael.

"That's owl poop," said Mom. "See these tracks with two toes pointing forward and two pointing back, and the owl pellets around the base of the tree?"

The Straight Poop

Some types of bird scat (also called guano) make good plant food. People buy bags of it to put in their gardens to make their plants healthy.

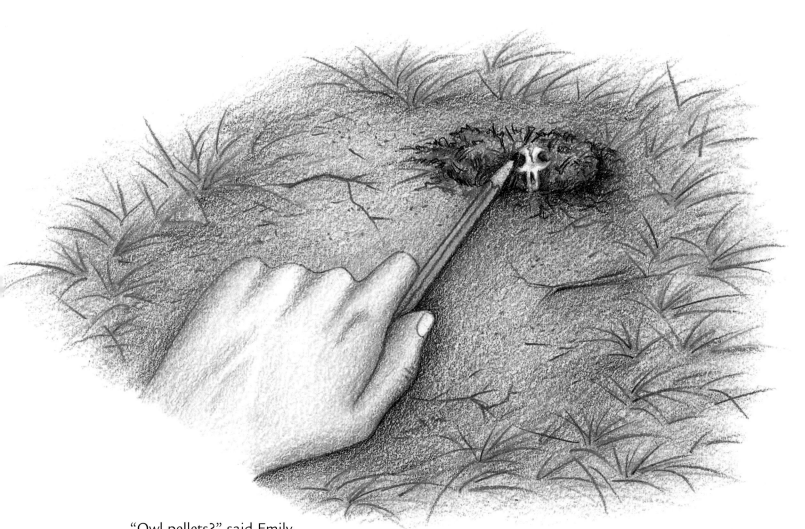

"Owl pellets?" said Emily.

"Owls eat their prey whole," explained Mom. "The parts they can't digest, like hair and bones, get coughed up in a pellet like this."

"Yuck!" said Emily.

The Straight Poop

Owls see very well at night, but they aren't blind during the day, like some people believe. They see just fine then, too.

"You can tell this was a big owl by the size of the tracks and the pellets," said Mom. "The bigger the owl, the bigger the owl pellets."

"There are a bunch of different owls in Rocky Mountain National Park," said Dad. "My favorite is the great horned owl."

"I like owls, too," added Mom. "But my favorite bird is the golden eagle. Let's keep our eyes open and see if we can spot one."

"Whoa, Dad! What happened to this tree?"

"Something was sharpening its claws. And if you look how high those scratch marks go, it was pretty big!"

"It's not just the animal that's big," said Emily. "Look at the size of this poop!"

"It looks like we found your black bear," said Dad. "Let's see what you learned today. What can you figure out about this bear?"

"It's as tall as you, and it has really long claws," said Michael.

"It's been eating plants," said Emily, "because there's no hair or bones in this poop."

"Good!" Mom said. "What else?"

Straight Poop

Black bears eat almost anything. They mostly live on leaves, nuts, berries, insects, twigs, and honey, but they also hunt small animals and fish.

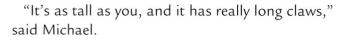

41

"Here's its footprint," said Michael. "It's really big, and it has more toes than a coyote or mountain lion."

"I told you you'd be able to count a bear's toes," laughed Dad.

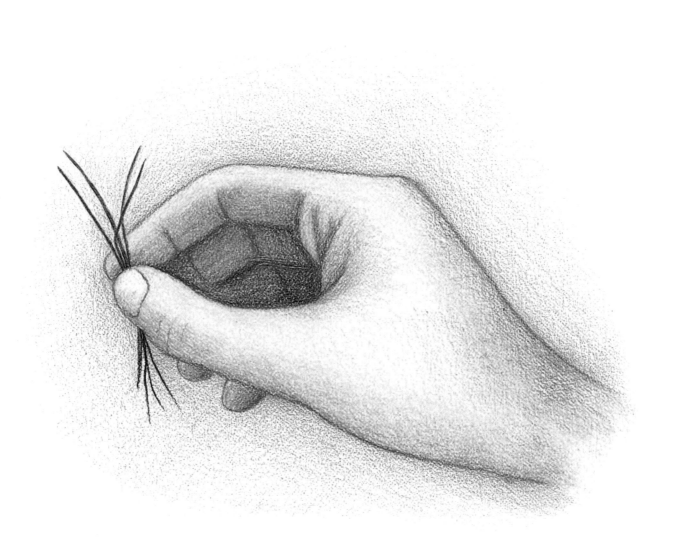

"It rubbed off some hair on the tree," said Emily. "You said this was a black bear, but these hairs are reddish brown."

"Black bears can be all different colors," explained Mom. "They can be black, brown, or cinnamon-colored, like this one. There are even black bears so light-colored they're almost white."

As they ate dinner that night, everyone talked about how much fun they had.

"We didn't see very many animals," said Emily, "but it seemed like we did."

"And I didn't get scared once," said Michael.

Tracks and Scat Notes

Bighorn Sheep
Hoofprints are straight along the sides, not curved like deer prints. Scat pellets usually have a dimple on one side.

Black Bear
Large tracks with five visible toes and claws. Scat changes depending on diet but usually contains vegetation.

Coyote
Tracks are like a dog's, with four toes, usually with visible claw marks. Scat is very dark colored with tapered ends and usually contains hair.

Elk
Tracks are longer and more blunt than those of deer. Scat is quite a bit bigger than a deer's.

Great Horned Owl
Tracks show four toes: two pointing forward and two pointing backward or sideways. Scat is runny and white. "Cough pellets" contain fur and bones.

Tracks and Scat Notes

Horse
Tracks are much bigger than deer tracks and are not split. Scat is in chunks, with roughage from vegetation often visible.

Marmot
Four toes on front foot and five on back foot. Scat is usually deposited on rocks and ledges.

Mountain Lion
Tracks are bigger than a coyote's, but claws don't show. Scat is rarely seen because they bury it.

Mule Deer
Pointy split-hoof tracks. Scat is long and oval-shaped like jelly beans, not round like a rabbit's.

Snowshoe Hare
Small tracks are filled in between the toes. Scat is in little balls.

The Author

Gary Robson lives in Montana, not far from Yellowstone National Park. He has written dozens of books and hundreds of articles, mostly related to science, nature, and technology. www.GaryDRobson.com

The Illustrator

Elijah Brady Clark has been passionate about design and illustration for as long as he can remember. After living his dream of traveling the United States in an Airstream Bambi Travel Trailer, he returned to northwestern Montana's Flathead Valley, where he grew up. He currently works as a designer and illustrator.

BOOKS IN THE
WHO POOPED?
SERIES:

Acadia National Park
Big Bend National Park
Black Hills
Cascades
Central Park
Colorado Plateau
Death Valley National Park
Glacier National Park
Grand Canyon National Park
Grand Teton National Park
Great Smoky Mountains National Park
Northwoods
Olympic National Park
Red Rock Canyon National Conservation Area
Redwoods
Rocky Mountain National Park
Sequoia and Kings Canyon National Parks
Shenandoah National Park
Sonoran Desert
Yellowstone National Park
Yosemite National Park